Caw'd ! Thas Sutten Good

Charlie Haylock

with cartoons by Barrie Appleby

To Derek
Keep a-troshin Bor!
Charlie Hay...
26·11·10

COUNTRYSIDE BOOKS
NEWBURY, BERKSHIRE

First published 2008
© Charlie Haylock, 2008

COUNTRYSIDE BOOKS
3 Catherine Road
Newbury, Berkshire

To view our complete range of books,
please visit us at
www.countrysidebooks.co.uk

ISBN 978 1 84674 124 1

*In memory of
Joyce and Gordon*

Designed by Peter Davies, Nautilus Design
Produced through MRM Associates Ltd., Reading
Typeset by CJWT Solutions, St Helens
Printed by Information Press, Oxford

Contents

PREFACE

DUE TO THE MANY REQUESTS I've had, and all the compliments from a great number of people, I felt I had to respond and write another book about this wonderful county of ours called Suffolk. I didn't need a lot of persuading, I can assure you.

So now we have a trilogy, *Sloightly on th' Huh*, followed by *A Rum Owd Dew*, and now the new rendition, *Caw'd A Hell! Thas Suffen Good*. 'Caw'd a hell' is a phrase widely used throughout Suffolk and, of course, means 'Well, I never' (or suffen loike 'at) and is not an expletive telling someone to go to the devil!

In the course of a year, with my one-man show, *An Eccentric Look at Suffolk*, I visit many theatres and village halls. I have numerous bookings for after-dinner speaking, and I have appeared on radio and TV – you might have seen me on *Bygones*.

But, wherever I go, I always get asked, by scores of people, this one question, time and time again: 'Why is it, that Suffolk people are asked so many times "What part of Australia are we from?"' I have answered that question in the chapter entitled *Are You Australian?*

I have written the book in a 'Suffolk yarn telling' manner, with humorous little Suffolk asides along the way, to make each story a compelling tale. This is interwoven with illustrations and superb cartoons by Barrie Appleby, the legendary cartoonist, whose simple style perfectly embodies the Suffolk 'hoomer'. However, one chapter alone, *Black Suffolk*, has deliberately been written with no humour at all. It is a gruesome, grisly account of a part of Suffolk history that should not be forgotten. Read it you must – but be prepared to be shocked!

The chapter *Suffolk Squit* captures the true Suffolk wit, with its droll deadpan punchlines. *Lorst in Suffolk* continues with the Suffolk 'hoomer' and concentrates on the fun we have when 'furreners' from other parts of the country get lost in the wilds of our countryside – 'furreners' who tend to ask the 'duzziest' of questions, usually with the rudest of manners. The other chapters include *Suffolk Landmarks* and *Suffolk Mysteries Solved*, and are perhaps a daring, cheeky but truthful look at familiar sights and established schools of thought, again with those searching Suffolk witty observations.

Dwile Flonking is a superb chapter on a Suffolk sport and pastime which, sadly, is slowly but surely disappearing. Another chapter deals with the ever-changing coastline of Suffolk and proves we must not be complacent – we don't want to go the same way as Norfolk!!! Caw'd a hell! No!

Why is Suffolk so important? Well, Suffolk is probably the most significant county in the evolution of the British Isles. The trilogy of books I have now had published, has looked at Suffolk's dialect, its history, things peculiarly Suffolk, landmarks, recipes, trades and industries, and many other subjects, all interlaced with that special brand of humour we call Suffolk squit.

Add that all together and the question as to why Suffolk is so important is readily answered, and 'thas suffen good'!

Charlie Haylock

ACKNOWLEDGEMENTS

I would like to thank the following people for helping me in my research for this book on Suffolk. Without their input, this book would not have been written. Special thanks must also go to all the staff at the three Suffolk Record Offices, especially Ipswich. They have been extremely helpful and supportive, and were never fazed by the amount of research material I was requesting. Thank you one and all.

Gordon Alecock Snr	Susan Keeys
Joyce Alecock	Laxfield Low House
William Alecock-McMahon	Laxfield Museum
Barrie Appleby	Sue Lodwick
Blyth Valley Dwile Flonkers	Long Shop Museum
Peter Carter	Long Shop Project Trust
Louise Clarke	Mr N. Longe
David Carruthers	Sally Looker
Garry Deekes	Audrey Lorford
Richard Deekes	Julia and Stephen Mael
Gavin Downes	Heather Marshall
Rory Downes	Kerry Meal
Edwardstone White Horse	Bruce Martin
Marian Eggett	Sue Munt
Dave Feakes	Eileen Nason
Maggie Grenham	Angela Plumb
Bridget Hanley	Ryes School
Deidre Heavans	Wendy Sadler
Maggie James	Saint Mary's Ewarton
Kentwell Hall	Walter Simpson
Alan (Caleb) Hall	Imani Sorhaindo
Bill Haylock	Geoffrey Smith
Ipswich Museum	Stradbroke Library
Maureen John	Stradbroke Millennium Trust
David Jones	Suffolk Records Offices

If I have missed anyone out, please let me know, and I will ask the publishers to include you in the next edition. It is purely unintentional with so many names.

Thank you kindly
Charlie

(Courtesy of the Long Shop Museum)

CAW'D A HELL – THAS SUFFEN GOOD!

(The Windmill House Collection)

Are You Australian?

WHEN SUFFOLK PEOPLE GO 'ABROAD' to Lincolnshire and, further afield, to places like Oxfordshire and Hampshire, the number of times they are asked, 'What part of Australia are you from?' are too numerous to count.

Indeed, even Suffolkers who have visited Australia on holiday, have reported, upon their return, that whilst they have been there they have regularly been asked, 'Whereabouts in Tasmania are you from, mate?' Apparently, Suffolk's dialect is closer to the Tasmanian accent, than that of mainland Australia.

I personally would like a pint of Adnams Best for every time I've been asked. When I went on a month's tour of south-west Ireland, not once was I asked what part of England I was from – it was always Australia.

It has its hairier side, though. Many years ago, when playing cricket against an Australian touring side, the very big, very fast opening bowler thought I was taking the micky out of his accent, although being Australian, he didn't actually use that particular phrase! I got peppered with short balls and bouncers. But it does go to show how close the dialects are.

Why? There is more than one reason. The widely-held belief that more people were sent out from Suffolk on the convict ships than from anywhere else is not all together true but the best part of a fair few were sent which did have a great bearing on the evolution of the Aussie dialect and helped shape it to what it is today.

Assisted Passage

There was also assisted passage and a deliberate Government policy to populate all the colonies throughout the 1800s, including Australia.

After the Napoleonic Wars, Suffolk knew extreme hardship amongst the lower classes. The population boomed and unemployment was rife. The government of the day decided that mass emigration would solve the problem and at the same time create townships and settlements in the colonies, which in itself would help the defence of those countries – a lot cheaper than sending out armed forces – Australia was to be no exception.

Advertisements appeared regularly in the *Suffolk Chronicle* and other publications, promoting emigration. On 20 February 1836 the Emigration Committee placed an advert in the *Chronicle* telling people who wished to emigrate to Van Dieman's Land that there would be a sailing from London on 23 April 1836.

> **Single females from 15 to 30 years of age, when approved by The Committee, will be allowed a free passage.**
>
> **Married mechanics and agriculturalists of steady character in great demand.**

Excerpts from an advert placed in the Blything Union read:

> **Australian exclusive of the conveyance to London under the Colonial Bounty Act**
> **For each person, 14 years old and upwards £1 - 0 - 0**
> **Children under 14 years of age 10s**
> **People desirable as emigrants:**
> **Shepherds and agricultural workers**
> **Female domestic and farm servants**
> **Young married couples with children**

The Emigration Committee were very strict on couples with children and, in their bid to create a population that would grow, once in Australia, they laid down the following guidelines:

> **The age of married couples, not having children above the age of IO yrs, is not to exceed 40**

A table was drawn up:

Couples 40 to 42, must be accompanied by 1 child over 10 yrs of age
Couples 42 to 44, must be accompanied by 2 children over 10 yrs of age
Couples 44 to 46, must be accompanied by 3 children over 10 yrs of age
Couples 46 to 48, must be accompanied by 4 children over 10 yrs of age
Couples 48 to 50, must be accompanied by 5 children over 10 yrs of age

The advert stated that suitable clothing must be supplied by the emigrants.

Men
Two suits outside clothing
Two pairs of strong boots or shoes
Eight shirts
Six pairs of worsted stockings
Three towels
2lb of marine soap, comb, etc
Women
Same with cloak and bonnet

A great many Suffolkers left for the Australian shores in this way. As Suffolk was one of the most densely populated rural areas at the time, it had felt the boom in population more than most. This resulted, possibly, in more people emigrating from Suffolk than from anywhere else.

Many settlements in Australia were named after Suffolk villages and towns, including Ipswich, Sudbury, Cavendish, Framlingham,

ARE YOU AUSTRALIAN?

Woodbridge, Lavenham and many more. There's even an island off Queensland called Stradbroke Island.

What About the Convicts?

It is fair to say that a great number of Suffolk felons and wrongdoers were sent over on the convict ships between the late 1700s and the 1860s. Some of the offences that were committed would not even get to court in this day and age, and the sentencing was harsh.

Nearly every parish throughout the county contributed towards this forced migration – obviously, Ipswich and Bury St Edmunds sent the best part of a tidy sum. Towns like Bungay, Framlingham, Hadleigh, Lavenham, Mildenhall, Stowmarket and Woodbridge also sent their fair share. There appear to be 'hotspots' – Sudbury, without a doubt, had proportionately more convicts than any other town. They certainly were an unruly lot – (nothing changes!). Nearly all the villages sent their quota in ones and twos, but once again there were pockets of unlawfulness. Places like Glemsford, Stradbroke, Assington and Kersey were perhaps even more unruly than Sudbury, and added to the list in great numbers.

Common surnames like Smith and Brown appear quite regularly in the records. But other surnames, not so common, appear more than most. There were a fair number of Nunns (not the religious kind) sent over; the Snells also appear frequently, as do the Simpsons.

A fantastic publication to study is *Transportees from Suffolk to Australia, 1787 to 1867* written by Richard Deekes. It names thousands of convicts sent from Suffolk, including the offence they committed, the court they were tried in, the sentence they were given, the name of the boat they went out on, when it left and arrived, and its destination. Obviously a great deal of research was conducted, compiling this compelling reference book. To me, what makes it stand out is the index, split into two, one for surnames and the other listing parishes and towns – it really does help anyone researching their unruly ancestors.

Unfortunately Richard died before the book was completed, but

ARE YOU AUSTRALIAN?

we should be more than grateful to his son Garry, who continued his father's work, and ensured it was published.

The following are excerpts taken from the book:

'Benjamin Hazelip was convicted at Ipswich Court, on the 5th August 1824. He was sentenced to be hanged, but was reprieved and transported to Australia for life, along with George Woodgate, Stephen Baldry, Thomas Barnaby and Israel Woodgate. All of them had broken into the dwelling house of Stephen Capon, and stole six sacks of white clover seed - with the sacks. [Marn't forget the sacks!]. Unfortunately Ben Hazelip died on the voyage on 21st July 1825.'

'Harriet Watson was convicted at Suffolk Quarter Sessions, Bury St Edmunds, on Boxing Day, 1829. She was sentenced to fourteen years' hard labour in Australia, for receiving duck stolen by Robert Cotton, knowing them to have been stolen from one Abraham Flack.'

(They obviously could not afford a Christmas dinner, and went out and got one. The sad thing is that there is no record of Robert Cotton being transported. One must therefore assume that he didn't see in the New Year. The duck might not have been strung up but it looks as if Robert Cotton was!)

'John Hammond was convicted at the Quarter Sessions, at Bury St Edmunds, on the 3 April 1829. He was sentenced to be transported for life. His crime was forgery - having altered an order to the keeper of the workhouse at Bury St Edmunds, from one Mr Pitcher, (one of the guardians) to twenty shillings, instead of half-a-crown.'

(In today's money, that's one pound instead of twelve and a half pence – scandalous – should be hanged!)

'James Nunn was convicted at Suffolk Assizes on the 2l July 1831. He was sentenced to be transported for life. He was charged with breaking into the dwelling house of John Nunn, a shopkeeper at Wattisfield, and stole 38 pairs of stockings, two pieces of calico,

twenty handkerchiefs, some cheese and some bacon. He was arrested in The Castle Inn in Bury St Edmunds, fast asleep and drunk.'

The sentencing was either 7 years, 14 years, 21 years, or life. However, occasionally, the judge would go decimal and dish out ten years. The reason behind the multiples of seven was quite simple. Seven years was the length of an apprenticeship, and these felons were starting a new career.

Although the sentencing was harsh and severe, it did not act as a deterrent. Just as much crime was going on nearly 100 years later. Times were extremely hard and poverty was everywhere. Crime was seen by many as the only way to survive, and a large percentage of the offences involved food and livestock. It is said that some Suffolkers actually committed a crime to get caught. They preferred to try their chance in Australia; they felt it would be less harsh than life at home in Suffolk. On the other hand, it is also said that some wrongdoers, when given life in Australia, requested to be 'strung up' and hanged.

This folk song was very popular in East Suffolk, and was a favourite of Geoff Ling, born 1916, from Blaxhall. His favourite 'singing pub' was the Blaxhall Ship.

Australia

When I was a young man,
And about seventeen,
I was all ready to fight,
For Victoria, our Queen.
But to keep her like a lady,
I went on that highway,
And for that,
I was sent to Australia.

ARE YOU AUSTRALIAN?

Australia, Australia,
How we worked hard in that land,
They drove us like horses,
To plough up their land.
You should have seen us poor fellows,
Oh! How cruel were they?
How hard is our fate;
In Australia.

Australia, Australia,
I shall ne'er see no more,
I met up with fever,
Brought down to death's door.
But if ever I should live,
To see seven years more,
I will then bid adieu
To Australia.

Margaret Catchpole

Without a doubt, the most famous transportee, who was sentenced twice to be hanged, and both times was reprieved to serve a term in Australia, was the infamous and celebrated Margaret Catchpole from Nacton.

As a young teenager, Margaret fell in love with William Laud, a free-trader (a respectable word for a smuggler). Some time later, William had been left for dead, after a skirmish with the customs men. Margaret tended to him and he recovered, although he was unrecognisable, with half his face having been cut away by the custom officer's sword. William continued his free-trading under a pseudonym, but was eventually press-ganged into the Royal Navy.

In 1797, Margaret was waiting for her loved one to return, when she was given word he was in trouble in London and needed her help. She instantly responded by stealing her employer's horse, a distinctive strawberry roan, and rode to London, dressed as a young man. On reaching London, she was apprehended, taken back to

ARE YOU AUSTRALIAN?

Margaret stealing the horse
(Suffolk Record Office, ref. HA213/1287/44)

Bury St Edmunds and tried. Horse stealing was a capital offence and she was sentenced to be hanged. This was commuted to seven years' hard labour in Australia, after pleas from the Cobbold family, her employers. As the 'waiting list' for transportation to Australia was so long, she languished in Ipswich gaol for quite some considerable time.

After two years of waiting, as fate would have it, she saw her lover, William Laud, in the debtors' prison next door. They were able to speak very briefly, and as he was preparing to be released, Margaret decided to escape and go with him. They met up and lay low at Orford but they were apprehended on the beach and William was shot dead, defending Margaret. On 6 August 1800, Margaret was convicted at Ipswich Assizes for escaping from Ipswich gaol. Again, she received the death penalty, but was reprieved once more and sentenced instead to be transported to Australia.

Once in Australia she turned out to be a model prisoner and became cook to the Commissioner General of New South Wales.

*Will Laud defending the injured Margaret on Orford beach
(Suffolk Record Office, ref. HA213/1287/42)*

Eventually she took up nursing and earned enough money to open a general store in Hawkesbury. Terrible floods were to devastate Hawkesbury and Margaret shew great courage and helped save many lives. Her written reports of the floods are the only eye-witness accounts in existence. In 1814 Margaret was given a pardon but stayed in Australia and carried on her nursing. She died in 1819 after contracting influenza from a patient.

Many stories and fables have surrounded Margaret Catchpole, and it can be difficult to distinguish truth from fiction.

The Australian Dialect

At the same time as all these Suffolkers were being sent out to Australia, quite a number went from Norfolk although not as many as from Suffolk. Norfolk people will readily tell you that's because they were a lot cleverer and never got caught. I cannot allow them to get away with that! It was because Suffolk was more densely populated. There was also a fair chunk from Essex, when that county had more of a country dialect, rather than the hugely London influenced one it has today. Cambridgeshire, Hertfordshire and Bedfordshire also made an input. These counties, with Suffolk as the driving force, would help fashion the Australian accent. All the dialects of these counties sound very different to the local ear, but to the 'furrener', they are extremely similar.

The other big contributory factor not mentioned thus far is the large number that went from East London – the Cockneys.

The Australian accent is very 'sing-songy', with sentences and phrases tending to go up at the end, making them sound like a question. This would be the equivalent of a mixture of the north Essex, Suffolk and Norfolk dialects, with north Essex and south Suffolk being sing-songy, and north Suffolk and Norfolk rising at the end of their phrases.

All dialects not only sound different but are also spoken in a different way. To illustrate the point – Scottish dialects are spoken with the teeth close together and the lips drooping slightly at the end, hardly opening the mouth at all. The sound is made from immediately behind the teeth – this is why the Scots can roll their 'r's. (It's not because of the way they walk!)

Cockneys tend to open their mouth wider and the sound comes from the front of the mouth. Add to this the fact that the Cockney dialect is most probably the fastest of all English speaking dialects, and you get the situation where the Cockney is unable to close his/her mouth quickly enough to make the 't' sound in the middle of a word. 'Butter' becomes *bu'er* and 'better' becomes *be'er*; this is called the glottal stop. It also means that sounds which require the tongue to be placed between the teeth are also impossible. So mother becomes *muvver* and 'through' becomes *froo*. 'Brother' becomes *bruvver*, sometimes shortened to *bruv*, and 'think' becomes *fink*.

The Australian dialect is also spoken with a wide-open mouth – so, cutting it down to simple basics, the Australian accent is a mixture of the lyrical East Anglian dialects (with Suffolk as the main contributor) spoken with the wide-open mouth of the Cockney.

CAW'D A HELL! THAS SUFFEN GOOD

Other parts of the country obviously sent their quota of convicts to these far distant shores, but they only had a minor effect on shaping the Aussie sound.

Many sounds the Suffolkers make in their speech are very akin to that of Australian. The common open *ay* sound as in 'make' (*mayke*), 'take' (*tayke*), 'day', 'sway' and 'Australian' (pronounced *Osstraylian*) is widespread in both dialects. Another example is the air sound, as in 'bear', 'care', 'fair', etc. There is also the hint of a double syllable when Australians pronounce words like 'here', 'dear', 'fear', etc., as *heeyer*, *deeyer* and *feeyer*.

There are many examples of these common sounds, and they are gradually increasing. What has taken Australia a couple of centuries to produce is happening here in Suffolk, and over a quicker period of time. Large housing estates, industrial areas and enterprise parks have been built in Suffolk – Great Cornard, Haverhill, Kesgrave, Martlesham and many more other places. The overwhelming (and I mean that in terms of numbers not character) outsider coming in is the Londoner, along with a great horde from south Essex. That London-Suffolk mix is happening all over again, and I think it's fair to say that, in future generations, Suffolk will sound more Australian than Australia.

I now hope you can understand why Suffolkers have been asked by so many people so many times, 'What part of Australia are you from?'

So, 'G'd Day fr'm Bungay ... Mayte!'

22

2
Suffolk Landmarks

AS PROMISED IN MY PREVIOUS BOOK, *A Rum Owd Dew*, I have taken another humorous look at some more Suffolk landmarks. There are some obvious ones, some that are not so obvious, some that should be, and some that need a bit of explaining. The captions show Suffolk 'hoomer' at its best, with that

Saxtead Mill (The Windmill House Collection)

Felixstowe Docks (The Windmill House Collection)

straight-faced logic. Even the supposedly illogical comments, when looked at closely, can provoke a sound and logical observation, sometimes exceedingly profound, as depicted in the Orwell Bridge caption on the front cover of the book. The humour shown at the crinkle crankle wall at Easton is an example of simple Suffolk logic overcoming a 'furrener's' arrogance. The caption to the 'Suffolk Trilogy', outside the Suffolk Showground, is to simply get in first, before Norfolk do – but I have recognised the Norfolk contribution though – as you will see later.

Saxtead Mill and 'Flixstowe' Docks, are just a bit of 'squit', and Laxfield Museum is just good honest fun.

The Crinkle Crankle Wall, Easton

Easton's crinkle crankle wall is the longest in the world. However, in 1973, part of it was in a bit of a state. The archives held at the

SUFFOLK LANDMARKS

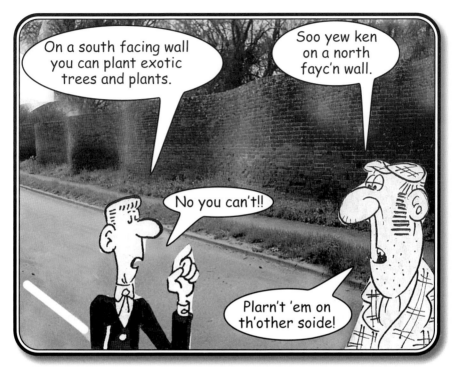

The crinkle crankle wall at Easton
(The Windmill House Collection)

Suffolk Records Office in 'Ipsidge', show that perhaps planners were none too bothered about the wall, although it is a listed building, and I quote, 'The remaining long stretches of serpentine wall to the north and east of the Park are in ruinous condition and not of special interest.' Huh! Not of special interest? Not only do we have something that's peculiarly Suffolk – we have a world record – the north-south stretch is 645 yards in length, and the east-west bit is 55 yards long – that's special!

Two famous individuals from the past, in fact, copied the style of this type of wall. Firstly, 'Capability' Brown, who designed the crinkle crankle wall at Heveningham Hall, and also, believe it or not, a crinkle crankle hedge at Chatsworth House in Derbyshire.

Secondly, a Mr Thomas Jefferson built crinkle crankle walls when landscaping the grounds of the University of Virginia, USA. Many Americans say he invented the idea, and Wikipedia calls them 'uniquely Jefferson'. Bloody cheek! He nicked the idea from Suffolk, and don't let anyone else tell you any differently.

Laxfield Museum

This is an utter gem – and yes, as the caption says, they do have a two-seater privy. The museum is an absolute must to visit. It's not just a show of exhibits – it actually takes you back in time. Each room is decked out and furnished in some period of time, and it's like stepping back in history. There's been input from the local school, and it shows. This museum is for everyone – for the grannies

The Old Guildhall, Laxfield (now Laxfield Museum)
(The Windmill House Collection)

and grandads, a trip down memory lane – for the youngsters, a realistic look into the living past. This comes highly recommended.

Edwardstone Hall

Now this is a little oddity in the Suffolk countryside, and the story that surrounds it is just as peculiar. You will have to read carefully because 'at dew git a bit complacayt'd'. Originally there was one Edwardstone Hall, the other side of Temple Bar, which goes back centuries. But it became a bit dilapidated and ended up a ruin. The goodly 'Lord of the Manor' moved out and into a large farmhouse, just this side of Temple Bar, and renamed his new place of residence Edwardstone Hall. A generation on or so, a decision was made to rebuild the old hall, and when completed, the family moved back in. The farmhouse that had been temporarily Edwardstone Hall was put up for sale, so it seems, as Edwardstone Hall. But when the purchaser moved in, the name had been

Temple Bar – Edwardstone
(The Windmill House Collection)

changed back to that of the original farmhouse, and the rebuilt hall had become Edwardstone Hall. The purchaser of the farmhouse appears to have been none too pleased, as they believed, so it's said, that they thought they were buying Edwardstone Hall. They changed the name of their farmhouse back to Edwardstone Hall, because that's what they had bought.

So we now have two Edwardstone Halls either side of Temple Bar, or do we? To add to the hilarity of the situation, a certain villager, Walter Simpson, put a 'grit owd' name plaque across his house saying 'Edwardstone Hall III', bringing much laughter and amusement to the villagers. Sadly it has been taken down and we are left with just two Edwardstone Halls – I hope you followed all that – but where else other than Suffolk would such a story unfold?

The Long Shop Museum, Leiston

This is truly a Suffolk landmark, and a tribute to the Garrett family who not only made an impact in the local area and throughout the

(Courtesy of the Long Shop)

British Isles, but became internationally famous. They put the Leiston Works on the world map. This is a fantastic place to visit – not only for the hundreds of workers that used to work at Garrett's when it was the biggest employer in the area, but for all generations, old and new. The atmosphere, the industrial smells, the exhibits and the helpful staff, should make you put this on your things-to-do list. Definitely!

The Suffolk Showground

Herein lies a story that not too many Suffolkers would admit to. At the entrance to the showground there are three sculptures depicting the 'Suffolk Trilogy'. No! Not Adnams, Greene King and Tolly's but the Suffolk Punch, the Suffolk Red Poll Cattle and the Suffolk Sheep. Trinity Park even derives its name from this famous trilogy. But as the caption says on the photograph (*overleaf*), they are all half Norfolk!

The Punch started its origins in south-east Norfolk and spread throughout both Norfolk and Suffolk, eventually becoming a pedigree breed of heavy working horse. One stable, in particular, comes to the forefront, in Ufford, just north of Woodbridge. All Punches today can be traced back through the male line to a stallion, Crisp's Horse of Ufford, foaled in 1768. It appears the Suffolk Punch was born.

The Suffolk Red Poll Cattle are 'chessnut' red, similar to that of a conker. They are a cross between the Suffolk Dun Cow, with a very high yield of milk, and the beefier Norfolk Red. Both were without horns, hence the name Poll(ed). The combined result of these two breeds means there is still a high yield in milk, and the beef is particularly tasty. The Suffolk Sheep is a cross between a Southdown ram and (yes, you've guessed) a Norfolk Long Horn ewe.

The *General View of the Agriculture of the County of Suffolk of 1797*, reports the Suffolk Sheep as 'having as mutton for the table of the curios no superior in texture or grain, flavour, quantity and colour of gravy, with fat enough for such tables.' The Suffolk Sheep Society

CAW'D A HELL! THAS SUFFEN GOOD

The Suffolk Showground, Trinity Park, Ipswich
(The Windmill House Collection)

was founded in 1886, by Edward Gittis of Snailwell. Perhaps we should blame him.

Therefore, should we really call it the 'Suffolk Trilogy', or own up? But who am I to try and change history?

Black Suffolk

THERE HAVE BEEN PEOPLE OF AFRICAN origin living in Suffolk since the 1500s. The earliest recording of a baptism comes later in 1634 in Sibton, that of Christianna Niger Anglice, 'a Blackamore'. We have seen the results of slavery, both in terms of the horrific experiences of those who were enslaved and the fortunes some Suffolk families made through their connection with slavery. We also have a champion who helped abolish this cruel and inhumane trade, and we have records of Black inhabitants integrating into village life, and being part of the community, in the mid 1800s.

During the1600s the slave trade had become established in the Americas and the Caribbean. Tobacco, rum, sugar and cotton were highly profitable commodities, even more so if you had a free labour force. At first, the native population were enslaved but because of new diseases they contracted, which they were not immune to, and through their inhumane treatment, this labour supply soon diminished. Plantation owners then used Irish prisoners of war and English convicts. The slave traders even went round and simply kidnapped the poor to meet the demand. But these people were not very productive. They were not used to the climate and they were inexperienced at growing these types of crops. At the same time, the number of plantations rocketed, and the demand for slaves soared. A new source had to be found – and Africa was the answer. Not only were the people there used to hot weather but they had experience of growing crops in that type of climate –

unfortunately that gave them the edge over their European counterparts. The Black African became the most sought after, and a very lucrative and most profitable trade began – for the traders and the owners that is!

The traders were nothing short of ruthless and had no thought for others, no matter who they were. The demand for ships' crews to man the slavers (ships that carried slaves), also dramatically increased. The recruitment drive to overcome this problem was to go into taverns and inns, or just round the towns and press-gang crew members. No negotiating whatsoever – physically overwhelmed and taken aboard – no telling the wife they wouldn't be home that night, or for the next two years or so.

Once they were at sea, the crew were cruelly and maliciously treated to keep them in order, and many died. Floggings were commonplace, not only as a punishment, but also as an example, as was keelhauling (being dragged all the way under the ship, from one side to the other).

It's hard to believe, but the Black Africans were treated even worse. The traders would go ashore and round up the native population – they were overpowered and taken aboard – anyone who put up a strong resistance was killed. Very quickly this barbaric way was adapted. The traders wheeled and dealed with the African chiefs and came up with an even worse practice. The chiefs didn't have a lot of choice – if they didn't comply – they ended up on a slaver with the rest of their people, or killed.

The 'slave triangle', as it was known, was an enormous money spinner. Ships from England, including Ipswich, would transport guns, gunpowder and alcohol to the African chiefs, who would help the traders with the supply of enslaved Africans. This led to warring amongst the tribes in their bid to supply the ever-growing demand. Once handed over, the slaves were chained, shackled, handcuffed, branded and transported to the Americas and the Caribbean in the most horrendous overcrowded conditions, as you can see from the diagram (*opposite*). Many died on this hellish journey. Some of the slaves were able to break free, only to jump overboard to a certain

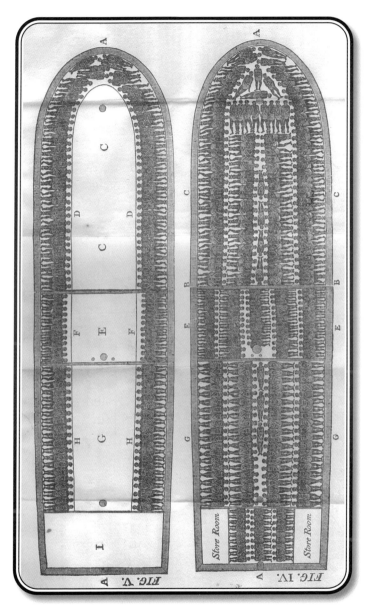

Diagram showing how the slaves were herded on board ship
(Suffolk Record Office)

death by drowning – they preferred to die rather than to be enslaved.

The lack of washing and toilet facilities were the least of their worries. They were treated severely and harshly, and the young girls and women were sought after, against their will, by the traders and sailors for their various pleasures. Once delivered to their destination, the slaves were sold at auction. The third leg of the triangle was to take tobacco, rum, sugar and cotton back to England, and the cycle would start all over again.

How was Suffolk involved?

Suffolk at the time was a very wealthy county and many rich people from Suffolk helped finance the slave trade. Many plantation owners found the conditions too hot and humid so they wanted to run their business from large country estates in England, and Suffolk was most sought after. The estates belonging to the Middletons, the Arcedeknes,

the Tollemaches, the Norths, the Longs and a host more, are attributable to the very large profits from plant-ations and slavery.

How else was Suffolk involved? Many rich fami-lies would have a black boy as a 'pet', and there was an advert in the *Ipswich Journal*, in 1786, 'for a place for a 14-year-old negro boy'. Sometimes kept on a collar and lead, dressed up in refined clothes, he would do his 'party tricks' for all to watch when guests come round. Hence the reason why we have 'Black Boy'

(Courtesy of Rory Downes)

pubs in Suffolk – at one time there was even a 'Black Girl' pub in Bury St Edmunds. (What I can't understand, in this age of political correctness, is why the black boys' faces on the pub signs have been replaced with the sooty faces of chimney sweep boys – haven't quite worked that one out yet.)

The ship builders of Ipswich built four slavers. The flint knappers from Brandon were exporting flints for the firearms being sent to the African chiefs. Suffolk merchants were sending out alcohol as well.

However, the general public did not profit one iota from slavery or its associated dealings – quite the reverse in fact. The rich were getting richer, and the poor were getting poorer, and by the early 1800s things were gravely desperate, as explained in *Are you Australian?* This led to the people revolting against the rich, either individually, in small groups, or in the full scale 'Bread or Blood Riots' of 1815 to 1816, (these riots occurred more in Suffolk than anywhere else). Slavery was seen as a way to only benefit the privileged few, and no one else.

The ordinary folk of Suffolk were starting to support the now-established 'Abolition of Slavery' movement. How had this movement become established? The main man is one Thomas Clarkson, who lived just outside Ipswich, at Playford Hall.

Thomas Clarkson

A great number of black Africans protested against being enslaved in many ways, and had a big impact on getting slavery abolished. It is fair to say, that Thomas Clarkson had heard these protests and is most probably the person who did more than any other, including the celebrated Lord Wilberforce, towards getting slavery abolished in this country. Black historians tend to agree with this statement, and hold him in high regard.

Clarkson had become aware of slavery while he was at Cambridge University. He submitted a paper in Latin on the subject of slavery and won first prize. In 1786, he translated the piece, *Is it Lawful to Make Slaves of Others Against Their Will?* into English for mass publication. His lifetime quest for the abolition of slavery had begun.

Thomas Clarkson (Suffolk Record Office, ref. PR/C/14)

In 1787 he was one of the founder members of the Committee for the Abolition of the African Slave Trade, and he became the committee's researcher. He interviewed over 20,000 sailors and obtained examples of the equipment used onboard the slavers – this took him two years to complete. The following year it was presented to a Privy Council Committee as 'The Present State of the African Trade' and Lord Wilberforce was persuaded to take it to Parliament.

Clarkson tirelessly continued to produce new evidence, including his 'Box', which contained examples of produce and fine goods grown or made by the African people. This was an attempt to dispel the belief that these people were nothing but savages. (It was the slave traders and the plantation owners who were the savages!) This evidence he made available to the general public through books and other publications. The evidence persuaded the ordinary folk to support his cause. An example is James Wright, a grocer in Haverhill, who stopped selling sugar in his shop.

In 1780 another committee was set up to look at the overcrowding on slave ships and eight years later an Act was passed to limit the number of slaves according to tonnage. However, the

ELECTORS
of EAST SUFFOLK.

GENTLEMEN,

HAVING heard that some of my friends wished me to declare in print, those opinions concerning the

ABOLITION
of SLAVERY

Which I expressed in my grateful address to the numerous and respectable Meeting at Wickham-Market. I come forward with pleasure to repeat those sentiments.

From the natural feeling of a free-born Briton, I *abhor* the idea of human slavery, and shall ever exert my best endeavours to promote the education and religious instruction of the poor Negroes, and to release them *when*, and WHEREVER it can be done with a prospect of improved happiness to *themselves*, and with *fair-handed brotherly justice* to our own countrymen ; and I trust, that from the humane measures lately adopted, and by the increased prosperity of our Colonies, that *happy time will soon arrive*, when every poor slave may obtain the blessing of freedom.

I have the honour to be,
GENTLEMEN,
Your obedient Servant,

CHARLES BROKE VERE.

BROKE HALL, *December* 5, 1832.

J. LODER, Printer and Bookseller, Woodbridge.

(Courtesy of Mr N. Longe, Suffolk Record Office, ref. HA24/50/19/4.4 (7))

traders didn't take much notice of this new ruling – they wanted to maximise their profits.

For a few years Parliament did not discuss slavery, and the movement to abolish it seemed to be running out of steam. But Clarkson was a fighter and he persuaded some MPs to re-open the case and, in 1807, on the third attempt, an Act was passed to abolish the slave trade. This was a step in the right direction, but slavery itself was still legal.

Clarkson was not satisfied and continued to crusade for the emancipation of slaves and, in 1823, he became Vice-President of the Anti-Slavery Society. For ten years he campaigned, getting more and more support, including that of Charles Broke Vere, M.P., from East Suffolk.

Finally, in1833, the Slavery Abolition Act was passed. This gave all slaves throughout the British Empire their freedom. This had taken Clarkson nigh on fifty years to achieve. At times he had pushed himself so hard that he had become very ill and at one point suffered a breakdown. But he would not give in until his goal was achieved. Thank you, Tom.

John Mattocks

Thanks to Richard Cobbold, the Rector of Wortham, we have an illustrated account of nearly everyone in his village. The work (four volumes) commenced in 1828 and continued for some forty years. He drew his own illustrations, which included John Mattocks, a man of mixed heritage. Bearing in mind this was in the mid 1800s it is interesting to read how the rector describes John's character, and how he overcame his drink problem. This insobriety could have stemmed from the fact that he was brought up in a pub in Stradbroke, where his father was the innkeeper. The rector's accounts always ended in a prayer, and John's was no different.

'What singular features and singular characters may be found in every parish in the kingdom, John Mattocks and his terrier dog were both characters in their way. John was a man of colour, his father was a genuine black man, and kept the White Hart Inn, Stradbroke. John's early occupation was that of a Huntsman to Squire Havers ... And John was a capital rider and understood horses well. John never fell except his horse fell with him ... he went to live with Squire Harrison at Wortham Hall. He became a most useful servant. John used to shave his master every morning and dress his wig, and also cut the young gentleman's hair...

'The family of the Harrisons were always good to Old John, and would not suffer him to come to want. They employed him in so

John Mattocks
(Suffolk Record Office,
ref. HD1025/2/49)

many ways according to his strength, and put up with the one foible which stuck to him until he became convinced that if he did not overcome it, it would conquer him and make him totally unfit for the Kingdom of Heaven. John was too addicted to drinking, but he did conquer the propensity and that from the conviction of the danger to his immortal soul. He did by the Grace of God entirely eradicate from his fleshly desires, the horrible propensity which had killed so many men before him.

'His wife was one of the fairest of her sex, very pale; but

John's family all partook of his dark features, although he had only daughters, no sons. His wife was the first to rejoice in John's altered habit and to acknowledge the goodness of God therein.'

'Though dark his face, his hands were clean.
'Tis God can change the heart.
Or would that no man were so mean
As with his love to part.
There's hope for John – he drinks no more.
No more to vice gives way.
At church he does his God implore
To wash his sins away.
There's hope, though foes against him rise,
That John may be forgiven,
Since greater than his enemies,
Is He who came from Heaven.'

History books tend to look at Suffolk simply as an Anglo-Saxon stronghold. That may have been the case in the first few centuries after the Romans left, and it is without a doubt the biggest influence which created a foundation and platform for Suffolk and 'Suffolkness' to evolve. Since those times we have had countless visitors from many parts of the world. Some were invited, some were not invited but invaded, and some were brought here against their will. Many different tribes, many different peoples and many different races have all helped to mould this county into what it is today. Suffolk has been constantly changing through the years, it has never stopped and it never will.

It was not until I completed my research that I realised for how long we have had black communities living in Suffolk – as early as the 1500s. I therefore feel I should amend the ingredients for my Suffolk cake mixture, which appeared in *Sloightly on th' Huh*.

BLACK SUFFOLK

5lb Angles
4lb Saxons
2lb Normans
1 pint Danes
2 tablespoons Jutes
2 tablespoons Frisians
3 teaspoons Vikings
1 teaspoon Celts
2 Romans beaten and whisked (vigorously)
Pinch of Dutch
2 tablespoons Black treacle
2 tablespoons Caribbean sugar

I think that makes the Suffolk cake look rather appetising and scrummy!

Ipswich Museum and Suffolk Records Office

Both these organisations have done a considerable amount of work to research this subject, and bring it to the attention of the general public. The Records Office in Ipswich has a permanent display dedicated to the work of Thomas Clarkson.

Since September 2007 the museum has had an exhibition on slavery – it is a permanent feature and well worth a visit. It shows how slavery started, how it continued, and how it was finally abolished. Some of the equipment exhibited is horrific.

Suffolk Squit

SUFFOLK **'HOOMER', ALONG WITH** that of our neighbours in Norfolk (as I've explained in my previous two books), is quite exclusive. This chapter, with its stories, cartoons and pictures, depicts that uniqueness. I have spent many an hour going through some wonderful photographic archives, both public and private and I've been able to select some 'interesting' scenes that immediately lend themselves to a comic caption. I hope you enjoy them as much as I did compiling them.

Suffolk 'hoomer' doesn't necessarily produce a swift response. In fact, it can take a fair few years before a timely retort is forthcoming.

(The Windmill House Collection)

(The Windmill House Collection)

The Farmer and His Sheep

ONE PEACEFUL DAY, DOWN ON THE FARM, a farmer was tending the sheep. It was the largest flock in East Anglia, let alone Suffolk. The tranquillity was brought to an abrupt end by a young man driving an off-road four-wheel-drive BMW thing, and screeching to a halt. The young man got out of the vehicle, wearing his Prada suit, his Gucci shoes, his D&G tie and his Dior sunglasses. Obviously not a country boy. Without saying 'good morning', or 'excuse me', or 'sorry to trouble you' (definitely a townie), he simply demanded that if he could tell the farmer the exact number of sheep in the field he would be entitled to take one for nothing.

The farmer slowly looked, weighed up the situation, and replied, 'Caw'd a hell bor – 'ere's hell 'n' awl in 'at 'ere medder. Yew're on.'

The young man takes out his Dell notebook computer, connects it to an Orange mobile phone, and surfs to a NASA page on the Internet, where he calls up a GPS satellite navigation system, to get an exact fix on his location. This he feeds to another satellite, which

(Laxfield Museum)

SUFFOLK SQUIT

(Laxfield Museum and the Low House)

scans the area in ultra high-resolution photo. Instantly he receives an e-mail on his Palm Pilot that the image has been processed and the data stored. The young man then accesses an MS-SQL database through an ODBC connected Excel spreadsheet with hundreds of complex formulae. He uploads all of this data via an e-mail and gets a response. He prints out a full-colour 50-page report (sounds a bit like Suffolk County Council!) on his hi-tech miniaturised HP Laser Jet printer. He then turns round to the farmer and tells him he's got precisely 873 sheep.

'Caw'd a hell! Yew're quoite roight! Best yew tayke one 'en.'

The young man then goes into the field and selects one of the animals, and puts it into the boot of his vehicle. He gets in and is just about to drive off, when the farmer say, 'Howd yew hard deeyer booy! If Oi tell yew, wot prafeshun yew are – 'n' Oi'm roight – 'en Oi'll hev ut back – but iff Oi'm wrong – yew ken tayke anuther bugger.'

'Okay. That's only fair. What am I?' was the young man's reply.

The farmer slowly looked at the young man, leant on his crook and say,

'Yew are a consolt'nt – a foinanshal consolt'nt – further more – yew're a foinanshal consolt'nt fr'm Lunnon.'

The young man was surprised, 'You are absolutely right – spot on. That was a lucky guess.'

'Guess be bugger'd! Yew dint guess th' nummer a moy sheep, 'n' Oi dint guess yew're a foinanshal consolt'nt fr'm Lunnon. Firster vawl – yew turn up owt th' bloo – no appointm'nt – when 'at's moost inconveenyant.' Seconnly – yew want pay'n fer an amser Oi awl reddy knew – tew a question Oi never arrs'd, 'n' thirdly – yew know bugger awl abowt wot yew're talk'n abowt.'

The farmer paused, 'Now give me back moy bluddy dog!'

(Laxfield Museum and the Low House)

The Floods

THE AREA BETWEEN SNAPE AND ALDEBURGH is exceedingly low lying, with marshes, reed beds and mud flats, with the river Alde meandering aimlessly along. The region is susceptible to flooding, and there have been some severe ones throughout history. At Slaughden Quay, just south of Aldeburgh, there is a wonderful 'owd sea dog' of a character who told me this tale. This retired fisherman had spent a lifetime at sea, and his weather-beaten face in itself could tell a story of its own. The strong, ruddy, round face had no hint of a smile but there was a glint in the eye.

This owd sea dog couldn't keep away from a life on the water, and went and got hisself a boat. He was now captain of his own vessel, conducting pleasure trips up the river Alde towards Snape and back. He told me that on one occasion, a rather wanting-to-know-it-all sort of gentleman came aboard, and immediately started telling passengers (and there were a fair few) to move around in order for him to be able to sit with his family all together.

About five minutes after cast off, this very loud passenger interrupted the captain's commentary and, in his booming voice, stated that some time ago the surrounding area had all been flooded, and asked the captain when that was.

'At be in nointee'n fifty three, when ...' He was rudely interrupted by this obnoxious character.

'No! No! No! Further back than that!'

'Yew must mean th' grayte storm in nointee'n twenty six when...'

'No! No! No! Further back in history than that!'

'Yew must mean th' grayte floods in sixtee'n hundred.'

'No! No! No! Much further back in history! Don't you know your history man?'

'Yew must mean jest arfter th' Oice Age when 'at awl melt'd.'

'Yes! Yes! Now when was that?'

'Caw'd A hell! 'At wuz a fair whoile agoo.'

SUFFOLK SQUIT

'Don't you know your local history, man? Can't you be more specific – more specific?'

'Well yes Oi dew, 'n' yes Oi ken. 'At wuz huppus foive on a Froidee arternoon.'

Fishermen repairing sails in Southwold
(Courtesy of Suffolk Record Office, ref. K 687/1/414/120)

Kentwell Hall (The Windmill House Collection)

(Courtesy of P. Carter and H. Woods)

SUFFOLK SQUIT

(Suffolk Record Office, ref. K/681/2/1/7)

(Courtesy of Audrey Lorford)

CAW'D A HELL! THAS SUFFEN GOOD

Auntie Hilda and the Outside Privy

AUNTIE HILDA HADN'T GOT AN INSIDE TOILET – not many people had. She had a privy down the bottom of the garden – just like everybody else. She was an old lady, and the sort that wore a hat on indoors. A visit to the doctor was unheard of – only if you were really poorly – and certainly not for something minor, or for 'suffen goo'n row'nd'.

Her nephew visited her one Monday morning and found his Auntie Hilda in the kitchen, bent up double and leaning on the kitchen table. The poor old gal was as white as a sheet and obviously in great pain.

'Wot an earth's th' matter Auntie Hilda?' he asked rather urgently.

'Caw'd a hell booy! Oi've bin bownd up fer a week,' came the agonising reply. With one hand leaning on the table, she pointed with the other, through the open window, towards the garden privy.

'Oi went dow'n 'ere larst Mundee. Oi sat dow'n 'ere fer an hour, nuthen! Oi went dow'n 'ere on Toosdee. Oi sat dow'n 'ere fer an hour 'n' a harf. Oi stroiv'd 'n' strayn'd but ought could Oi parss.'

'Oi went dow'n 'ere on Wensdee. Oi sat dow'n 'ere' fer tew bluddy hours, Oi grunt'd 'n' grown'd. Not a sossidge!' she said with a pained expression.

'As th' week's gone on 'at's got wusser 'n' wusser!' The tears were filling her eyes.

'Oi went dow'n 'ere 's'morn'n 'n' caw'd a hell booy, Oi sat dow'n 'ere fer oover forwer sodd'n hours!'

'Auntie Hilda, yew ought a tayke suffen.' the nephew insisted.

'Oi did! Oi did! Oi took moy knitt'n!'

Sunday morning just before church (Snape – 1920)
(The Windmill House Collection)

Bellringers on Saturday – Bury St Edmunds
(Suffolk Record Office, ref. K/681/1/81/277)

Bellringers on Sunday – Bury St Edmunds
(Suffolk Record Office, ref. K/681/1/81/276)

SUFFOLK SQUIT

(The Webb Collection)

Dad's Forgotten Cap

THIS IS A TYPICAL SUFFOLK ONE-LINER that reverses the situation.

I was having a drink with some of the family, including my father, in my local. There was the best part of a fair few all locals – all having a good time. The jovial atmosphere started to get a bit strained. A 'furrener' had entered the throng and, within a short space of time, had started to take over. The sort that talks in a very loud voice and, although he had been in the place just a few minutes, was speaking to the locals on very familiar terms, as if he had known them all his life (not recommended in a Suffolk pub full of locals).

My father had an early start next day and decided to walk home. He bid farewell and went out the door. However, he had left his cap on the hook. About five or ten minutes later, my father re-entered and went to take his cap from the hook. A big booming voice came across the room – the 'furrener'. 'You had too much to drink! Ay! Ay! You forgot your cap didn't you?'

My father slowly put his cap on his head and replied, 'No moy deeyer booy, Oi remembered ut.' and walked out the door amidst great laughter and one very red face.

5

Suffolk Mysteries Solved
(Or are they?)

THERE ARE MANY MYSTERIES IN SUFFOLK (I could be one of them, I suppose) that have many stories surrounding them, some true, some not so true, some made up and some just unexplained. I have researched a few, and not necessarily the most obvious ones.

Holy Trinity Hospital, Long Melford

This must rank as one of my favourite mysteries because I like to keep history and tradition alive and, with that in mind, when I get to my dotage, this is where I would like to be housed – to carry on the traditions of previous occupants.

This is known locally as 'Spite House' and is situated on the green at Long Melford, just by the entrance to the church grounds. It is said, because of its name, to have been built in the late 16th century when there was a big dispute carrying on between the owners of Kentwell Hall and the owners of Melford Hall, just down the road. This dispute got to such proportions it is rumoured that the Kentwell Hall faction, out of spite, had this building erected in such a place that it would mar the view of the church from Melford Hall. This is not the case. In fact it was Sir William Cordell from Melford Hall

Spite House, Long Melford
(Courtesy of William Alecock-McMahon)

who had the building erected in 1573. It was an almshouse, but 'almshouse' was not a particularly posh name, so it was called the 'Hospital of the Holy and Blessed Trinity'. It quickly became known as 'Hospital House', which the locals would have pronounced as 'Spital House', and this got shortened to 'Spite House'.

The building was erected *'to provide shelter for elderly residents, some of whom might have to endure severe hardship and deprivation, particularly if they have no families to care for them.'*

'It was to be a peaceful and comfortable haven for the elderly, each of whom will live out the remainder of their days in religious devotion, free from burden of all material worries.'

The last quote shows why it was built so near to the church – the residents could not have an excuse for not attending. The statutes and the ordinances of the almshouse were drawn up and it would

Melford Hospital 1865. Standing (L to R) Gooch, Rivers, Olley, Lyng, Death, Howe, Perry, Cadge. Sitting (L to R) Knapp, Howe, Halls, Lorking. (courtesy of the Trustees of Holy Trinity Hospital)

house twelve brethren, one governor and two widows. It stated how the brethren were to be selected and laid down the criteria as to whom should be chosen – all from Melford and the immediate surrounding area.

The eleventh of the statutes stipulated the qualities that the widows should have – and it really does go to show what a 'man's world' it was:

> *'There shall be chosen two honest widows of good conversation and honest fame of the age of fifty years at least, the same to be provided within the town or parish of Melford or nigh thereabouts with the consent of the warden and most part of the brethren,*

whereof the one to be the Butler and Laundress, the other Cook and Dairywoman, and either of them to have special care of the aged, sick, or impotent, and both of them to help and join together in brewing and baking for the said poor.'

In short, they were going to wait hand and foot on the brethren and Governor, and tend to all their needs, (and I mean all their needs by the sound of it). In return they got free accommodation.

Not very long after its opening, there were all sorts of complaints from the near neighbours, and I quote,

'Governor, Many complaints have come to me of your house, both of your selfe and most of the brethren, as in tipling, wenching and in suffering your said brethren to take their owne pleasures in goeing up and downe as they list themselves, contrary to the statutes and ordinances of the house.'

Now you can see why I would like to end my days in such a place – I hope things haven't changed!

Through the ages, many scandals followed and, in 1878, Sir William Parker from Melford Hall expressed his concern about improper conduct and insubordination, and that 'misconduct among the brethren did sometimes occur'. (Fantastic! – I haven't been put off yet.) So if my two sons are wondering where to put me – don't wonder any more!

The Low House, Laxfield

This is another of my favourites and again, you'll see why. The proper name for this unique 15th-century hostelry is the King's Head. When you go through the front door, it's like going through a time warp. The place has not been refurbished since 1896, according to one of the past landlords, it has only been decorated, and it now has electric lights. The old settles are still there, as is the fireplace with all the 'owd gubbins' for cooking, although it is not

The King's Head pub (Laxfield Museum)

now used for cooking I hasten to add. There are three separate drinking rooms, plus a restaurant, but there isn't a bar – the ales and beers are still sold from the back kitchen.

This is a living and vibrant 'museum' with all the atmosphere that goes with such an historic landmark. Highly recommended! At the time of writing, the present landlady is the granddaughter of Mr and Mrs Felgate who kept the Low House from 1882 to 1943. Their son Thomas took over in 1943, after the death of his father.

Why 'The Low House'? There are three theories put forward. Firstly, during the time of the English Civil War, the followers of Oliver Cromwell and his Roundheads would have been 'Low' Churchers, and whilst they shouldn't drink (but they did) they couldn't be seen in a place called the 'King's Head' so it was nicknamed the 'Low House'. It's rumoured that the Royalist supporters drank in the other 15th-century pub in the village.

Secondly, it's been said it was so named after the type of clientele

A previous landlord and landlady, Ron and Dot Read,
posing in the back kitchen of the Low House
(The Low House)

who used to frequent the place – not now I hasten to add – and that it was a den of iniquity.

The obvious reason for me is quite a simple one and is widely held to be the real one. The other pub is up the hill, and 'the Low House' is down the bottom of the hill, by the stream – that to me makes it 'the Low House', but go and see for yourself, and make your own mind up – you won't be disappointed.

St Mary's church, Ewarton

This church was frequented by no lesser royal personage than Anne Boleyn while she was visiting her favourite aunt and uncle at Ewarton Hall.

This grand hall was erected in Tudor times, and built to face the estuary. The use of red brick was revolutionary at the time, an innovation. The tunnel gateway is square with a vaulted ceiling and all the elevations are symmetrical. Anne fell in love with Ewarton and always said that, upon her death, she would like her heart to be buried in the church. Well, death came sooner than she thought, and Henry VIII had her tried for adultery (as if he hadn't indulged). She was found guilty and was sentenced to death. After she was beheaded, she was wrapped up and put in an unmarked grave.

Ewarton Hall and Gateway
(The Windmill House Collection)

CAW'D A HELL! THAS SUFFEN GOOD

Whether her heart was cut out or not and brought to Ewarton has not been recorded.

But – yes – but … Joseph Amner, who had been sacristan of the church for 50 years takes up the story.

> 'I was in the church with stone masons and carpenters helping to finish up the job – that was in 1836 – when the architect who was there gave orders that the south wall in the chapel should be made good where there was a bulging out. The masons started work and very soon came upon a leaden box covered with lime and dust. We were ordered to open it, but there was only a little black dust in it and it was soldered up again and placed on a coffin in the vault in the Lady Chapel. And if the vault was opened up again I could at once find it. My grandfather always told my father that old men and women in the parish had told him, as their parents had told them, the Queen's heart was in the church and would be found some day or other. So directly I saw the lead box I said to them all, "That's just what my grandfather told my father and my father told me, it was the truth."'

Has Ewarton really got the heart of a queen? If not, they've got her head instead – the Queen's Head pub, so called after Queen Anne Boleyn herself. But shouldn't it be the Queen's Heart?

Freston Tower, Freston

This is an odd one, and the more I learnt about this one the less I knew. Nobody knows its purpose or exact date of construction – however, we do know that it's Elizabethan.

It does have some rather unusual architectural features. It's built of red brick with blue diapers, (amazing what they used for building materials in them days). The diapers are deliberately over-burnt bricks put into a pattern with the red bricks. This occurs on the north and west elevations because it would be visible from the river, which would have had a great deal more traffic than the 'Ipsidge' to Shotley bridle path.

SUFFOLK MYSTERIES SOLVED

Freston Tower
(The Windmill House Collection)

There is one room per floor, and the staircase hugs against the north wall rising six storeys and opening onto the roof with an arcaded parapet. There are polygonal buttresses at the four corners which rise into finials. There are 26 windows plus 7 blanked ones. They become more grandiose and elaborate as the tower rises. The windows at the top floor are the grandest with six lights separated by transoms. The triangular pediments to the windows on the top three floors were very avant-garde in their day.

Legend has it, that the tower was built for the education of the beautiful Ellen de Freston in the late 16th century. She was supposed to have studied a different subject each day, on each floor – hence the six floors.

> Monday she studied charity – first floor
> Tuesday she studied tapestry – second floor
> Wednesday she studied music – third floor
> Thursday she studied painting – fourth floor
> Friday she studied literature – fifth floor
> Saturday she studied astronomy – sixth floor
> Sunday attendance at church – hence no seventh floor

Another theory is that it was built purely as a folly, as an indication of wealth (hence all the fancy architecture) to coincide with Elizabeth I's visit to 'Ipsidge' in August 1579. Remember, at this time, Suffolk was the wealthiest county in England, and had been so from Anglo-Saxon times. It was also the most densely populated. I'll let you decide – but the history continues.

The tower changed hands several times and in 1765 it was advertised as a treatment centre for smallpox – patients had to provide their own tea and sugar, and were charged between three and six guineas a week.

By 1771 it had become an inoculation centre for the disease, and that takes me on to the next point. Freston, and the surrounding villages, was the centre for the last epidemic of the plague in England – from 1906 to 1918 – (yes, 1906 to 1918), time we were moving on.

Martello Tower, Slaughden

This is a unique Suffolk landmark. But why was it built in that location, when all around are mud flats and marshes? Why is it the largest one built, why is it the most northerly tower, and why is it the only clover-shaped tower in the country?

Martello towers were built in the early 1800s as protection against an invasion from Napoleon Bonaparte. They were built along the south coast, and along the shores of Essex and Suffolk. The design, ironically, was taken from a similar tower built on

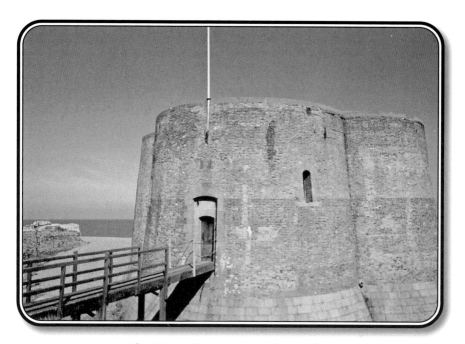

The Martello tower at Slaughden

Mortella Point in Corsica which, in 1794, withstood a British Navy bombardment. Corsica is where Napoleon was born.

Usually the towers were round with stuccoed walls, tapered to deflect cannon shot. The walls were 13 ft thick on the seaward side. The basement was for provisions, ammunition and gunpowder. The first floor was a garrison for 24 men and one officer – the officer's quarters were equivalent in size to that of the men's (well, he did have his reports to write and needed somewhere to file them). The upper floor was the gun platform, which was reached by a stairway built into the wall. The gun was normally two and a half tons and fired 24-pounders a mile out to sea. There were no latrines, so you went outside (amazing what they put down that there gun – no wonder we won. What you did when under siege … I don't know).

In the early 1800s Slaughden was a thriving community, not like it is today. It was a vibrant port and an immensely important place to defend both strategically and economically. That's the reason why it was built. Most probably it was more important than anywhere else along the Suffolk coast at the time. That's why they didn't build any more towers further north.

Napoleon could have attacked Slaughden either from out at sea or by coming up the river from Shingle Street. Therefore the tower had to defend both sides, not just the seaward side. That is why we have the clover-shape design. Work started in 1806, and millions of bricks were unloaded onto the beach. It was originally budgeted to cost £1,000, but 'due to rising costs and unforeseen complications' the eventual costs more than doubled and was under much discussion and opposition in Parliament. (Some things just never change – where have I heard this all before? Millennium Dome, London Olympics, etc. You'd have thought they would have got it right by now – wouldn't you?)

The building work stopped in 1812, and the tower was left not quite finished. We had beaten Napoleon at Waterloo, and he was no longer a threat. The tower was restored at a later date.

It's rather ironical – what Napoleon couldn't achieve, the sea eventually did – and Slaughden was practically wiped off the map.

Lorst in Suffolk

ONE SUBJECT THAT'S PARTICULARLY AMUSING to the Suffolker is the lack of propriety sometimes displayed by 'furreners' wanting directions, after they have lost their way in the Suffolk countryside. The responses to these often rude interruptions to our peaceful and gentle world are tried and tested – much to our

(Suffolk Record Office, ref. K681/2/78/52)

own amusement, leaving the strangers even more bewildered than they were before. What adds to the flavour is that they are always in a hurry, and we just like to take our time, 'noice 'n' steddy'. I have included one of my monologues depicting such a scene, around Lindsey, a village that had two pubs, both called the Rose, one red and one white. This causes much confusion to the 'furrener'. It stems back to the days of the Wars of the Roses, and the good folk of Lindsey thought they'd hedge their bets.

If only they would ask us politely – but I suppose if they did we wouldn't have so much fun. One cartoon, in particular, shows the annoyance of one 'owd' Suffolker to the apparent rudeness of the visitor.

This chapter is centred around the droll replies of the locals, but I've also included other humorous responses to transport generally.

(Suffolk Record Office, ref. K681/1/237/68)

LORST IN SUFFOLK

(Suffolk Record Office, ref. K681/1/237/62)

(Suffolk Record Office, ref. K681/2/78/51)

CAW'D A HELL! THAS SUFFEN GOOD

(Suffolk Record Office, ref. K681/2/78/69)

(Suffolk Record Office, ref. K681/2/78/70)

LORST IN SUFFOLK

Lorst in Suffolk

Lorst in Suffolk, 'n' yew doon't know where t' goo.
Stonham Parva, Thornham Magna, Thorpe Morieux,
Swingleton Green, Rickinghall Superior 'n' Sutton Who?

A treasure hunt had been sorted out,
By a motoring club, from somewhere afar,
Looking for clues, as they charged about,
Racing around Suffolk, in their flashy sports cars.

Lavenham was en route, but the locals weren't told.
So what happened that day – will slowly unfold.
'Bugs' and 'Waffer' were strolling along,
Whistling and singing the Ploughboy Song,
Mardlen and jo'en, without a worry.
When a sports car pulls up – in a davil of a hurry!

'Hey! We want your help – we're terribly lost!'
'Rum funny thing t'say,' say Bugs, 'Yew're heeyer a-course.'
'Now iff yew wuz t' tell uss where yew be a-head'n,' say Waffer,
'At'll be a diffrent matter awl t'gather.'

'We're looking for clues – the others are chasing.'
Bugs scratched his head and looked deliberately dumb.
'Dew yew want t'goo th' way yew're face'n?
Or turn row'nd, 'n' goo th' way yew've come?'

'We're looking for Lindsey Rose,
Does she live round here?'
'At little mawther no-one knows.
But we know of tew 'at are fairly neeyer.'

'Fust 'n' foremost,' say Bugs, 'Lindsey Bottom Rose.'
' 'N' secondly,' say Waffer, 'Is Lindsey Top Rose.
One is red 'n' th' other's whoite.
Tell uss which one, 'n' wee'll soon put yew roight.'

'Either will do!' came the impatient reply.
Bugs and Waffer gave a concentrated sigh.
'Up t' th' top heeyer, 'n' tayke a left.' – 'Roight?'
'Dow'n t' th' bottom 'n' tayke a sharp roight.' – 'Roight?'
'Tayke second left, afore yew git t' th' bridge.'
'Goo any farther 'n' yew'll end inner ditch.'

'Up th' hill, 'n' dow'n th' other soide.'
' 'N' heeyer th' layne ent very woide.'
'With any luck 'n' Oi suppose.'
'Yew'll now be face'n th' Lindsey Top Rose.'
'Wee'll keep an oye owt fer all 'em others.'
' 'N' jest loike yew – 'ay'll goo row'nd Will's mother's.'

'How far is it?' their patience is starting to crack.
' 'At seven moile 'ere, 'n' seven moile back,'
Say Bugs with a glint in his eye, 'At's roight bor.
But in 'at little sports car, yew'll do ut in forwer!'

Lorst in Suffolk, 'n' yew doon't know where t' goo.
Stonham Parva, Thornham Magna, Thorpe Morieux,
Swingleton Green, Rickinghall Superior 'n' Sutton Who?

Charlie Haylock

Dwile Flonking

World Champions!

This ancient Suffolk sport first started in the 8th century as a ritual after harvest. Its origins are attributable, so it's believed, to King Offa, an Anglo-Saxon king. Through the ages, dwile flonking gradually changed, and by the mid 1500s, had also become a sport. Matches between opposing teams would take place after harvest, and the season would run up to Christmas.

By the mid 20th century, dwile flonking had become purely a sport, but was still played after harvest, even though the ritual side of things had disappeared. Although the World Championships have ceased, the game is still occasionally played, usually as a spectacle at charity fund-raising events.

The Blyth Valley Dwile Flonkers are the reigning champions of the world. Unfortunately, though, the last World Championships were held in 1970 in Beccles. (It must be revived!) The World Cup, a pewter chamber pot is currently housed somewhere in Halesworth.

The rules may have altered through the centuries, and it may have gone from a harvest ritual to a sport, but there has been one common theme throughout that has never altered (and I hope it never does!). From the days of King Offa, to the present day, the principal object was to get 'hammered' – to consume vast quantities of the very best Suffolk ales.

The term 'dwile flonking' literally means 'floor cloth flinging'.

The World Cup
(courtesy of Alan 'Caleb' Hall & Blyth Valley Dwile Flonkers)

'Dwile' comes from 'dwiling' – the Old Dutch for a coarse flannel material, knitted together to resemble a closely woven net cloth. You will see from the rules shown on page 80 that we have kept alive old Suffolk dialect words that otherwise would have been forgotten. Words like 'driveller', 'swadger', 'girting' and 'morther' readily come to mind, and are explained quite simply and accurately in the rules, as revived by the Waveney Valley Dwile Flonking Association.

Before proceedings commence, both teams together, must sing the game's traditional song. It is also sung at the end of the match, but this time, nobody can understand the words.

Here we em be together
(The Dwilers Song)

Now here we'm be boys,
Now here we'm be.
With our Dwiles an our Drivellers,
Dwile Flonkers are we.

DWILE FLONKING

Now you know how to play boys,
So hear what I say.
Grab hold of that Driveller,
And shout, 'Dwiles away'.

Now down we do get,
To the old village green,
The Flonking match there,
Is for all to be seen.
Old Tom scores a Ripper,
An' the crowd they do shout,
Then they start a-hullin
Them dishcloths about.

Now the game it do end,
An' then down go the sun,
An' one team ha lorst it,
While the other has won.
But nobody knows,
Of the score on the board,
Cos they're flat on their backs,
An' as drunk as a lord!

Now you seen how the game go,
An' you know how to play,
So join in the chorus,
An' shout, 'Dwiles away'!
So cheerio now,
To the old village green,
An' we'll come back next year,
Wi' a far better team.

Amos Thirkle

Dwile Flonking

As revived and played by
The Waveney Valley Dwile Flonking Association

This ancient Suffolk game is thought to be a kind of harvest ritual. The game is believed by experts to be about 400 years old.

EQUIPMENT

Dwile—This is a type of dishcloth, resembling a net.
Driveller—A pole used to project the dwile.
Chamber Pot—The use of this will be explained later in the rules.
Flonker—This term applies to the person who projects the dwile.
Barrel or Bucket—This must contain English ale.
The action of projection is known as *flonking*.

DESCRIPTION

Each team consists of eight or more players. These players form a circle around one of the opposing team. When the referee gives the traditional shout of "Here y'go t'gether," the man in the circle takes a dwile from the bucket of ale and places it on the end of his driveller.

So, with his driveller and beer-soaked dwile the encircled man shouts, "dwiles away!" and then proceeds to spin round. With a flick of his driveller, he attempts to project the dwile towards the circle. He flonks two dwiles. If he scores with both attempts he receives a bonus flonk.

While the man in the middle is spinning round, the circle may move round and up and down, but may not break the circle. This action is known as *girting*.

Scoring is as follows:

Wonton—This term applies when the dwile strikes one of the encircling team on the head. It scores *three* points.

Morther—When the dwile strikes a player on the chest. It scores *two* points.

Ripper—A hit below the belt. It scores *one* point.

Swadger—This term applies when the dwile hits none of the men in the circle. If this happens, the referee shouts, "Swadger," and the following takes place:

The circle moves back and forms a straight line. The flonker who "swadged" is then handed a chamber pot containing English ale. Directly he starts to drink the ale, the dwile is passed along the line of opposing players. At the same time, the latter utter the ceremonial chant of "pot, pot, pot...."

If the flonker fails to consume the contents of the receptacle by the time the dwile has been passed along the entire line his team loses one point.

The entire procedure of the game is then repeated by the other team.

WINNING

The team with the most points wins the match, an extra point being added to a team's score for every man still sober.

REFEREE

As in every sport, the referee's decision is final, and he has the right to send any player off the field.

N.B. Before and after each match the teams sing the traditional game's song: "Here we em be together."

Finally, by way of tradition, the teams should turn out in Yokel attire.

DWILE FLONKING

The World Champion Dwile Flonkers 1968.
Back row (L to R) 'Gaffer' Lee, 'Caleb' Hall, 'Jeremiah' Barham,
'Fiddler' Warne, 'Yiddle' Smith.
Front row (L to R) 'Woody' ?, 'Dorset' Denny, 'Mac' MacBumey,
'Boozie' Took, 'Dunker' Maulden (holding the pot), 'Wudger'
Deare, 'Whistler' Gooch. Two flonkers unable to get to the photo
session – I wonder why? – are 'One-Up' Ulph and 'Spud' Bird.
All the team are still alive today, except for 'Wudger',
who has sadly passed away.
(courtesy of Alan 'Caleb' Hall & Blyth Valley Dwile Flonkers)

The game usually consists of two innings (if you can last that long). It is now custom and practice for the two teams to attire themselves in traditional yokel dress, as you can see from the victorious team photo of the Blyth Valley Dwile Flonkers.

'Yiddle' Smith is holding the driveller with a beer-soaked dwile on the end, and 'Dunker' Maulden is holding the pewter chamber pot, which is full (not for long) of Adnams Best.

This game must be revived! Does anyone want to start up a league? What started off as a ritual, some twelve centuries ago, and continued as a sport for nigh on 450 years, must not be lost. It's organised binge drinking done sensibly, and no one gets hurt, (apart from the next morning that is). Someone contact me please!

The Changing Suffolk Coast

MANY TOURISTS VISIT OUR COASTAL VILLAGES, nature
reserves and resorts, but do they realise how much it has all
altered? Through the centuries, the Suffolk coastline has continually
changed. It has taken a 'helluva' pounding from the North Sea, and
communities have been lost or have practically disappeared. On the
other hand, some coastal features have grown and, with man's
influence, some of our wide-open estuaries have been turned into
farmland.

Dunwich

The most famous lost settlement along the Suffolk coast (and
probably in the whole of England) is at Dunwich. It is now a very
tiny village, with a popular fish and chip shop very close to the sea,
famous ecclesiastical ruins, a 'couple a three' houses, a few
fishermen's black huts and a dinky little museum. The latter is an
absolute 'must' to visit – you'll be enthralled and find it difficult to
leave. History comes alive here, and you can feel the strange
atmosphere of a lost city. I only hope that 'grit owd' anchor outside
the museum keeps it in place, and that it 'ent' washed out to sea.

Back in Anglo-Saxon times, it was a completely different story.
Dunwich was the capital of East Anglia and one of the biggest ports
in England, with a quay, fishing vessels, coastal vessels, fair ships
and warships.

In about AD 630 King Sigebert brought Felix, a Burgundian
bishop, onto the scene and the first church was built. Later Edward

the Confessor had a church built, William the Conqueror had two, and through the centuries, many more churches and monastic buildings were erected (Suffolk Coastal District Council would have had a heyday with all that planning permission).

By the 1200s things started to go wrong – coastal erosion began to have an effect. Dunwich's importance as a port was starting to decline and, in Edward I's reign, the fleet had been reduced to 16 warships, 20 trading vessels, and 24 fishing boats. In 1347 (a very bad year) after the Siege of Calais, not only did Dunwich practically lose all its warships, but she lost 500 (yes – five hundred!) of her townsmen. During the 1600s and 1700s the North Sea was hitting Dunwich with a vengeance. After the storms of 1677 the sea had reached the market place and during a series of 'attacks' thereafter, St Peter's church was lost to the seas, as were the town hall and gaol. In 1740 a great north-easterly gale did untold damage and even washed away the 40-ft high Cock and Hen hills.

It is estimated that over a mile of coastline has gone, and under the sea you'll find the remains of ten churches alongside umpteen chapels and monastic buildings (shoals of angel fish a plenty – no doubt).

Aldeburgh, Thorpeness and Slaughden

('Where's Slaughden?' I hear you say.)

Not many people know, but Aldeburgh has also had its fair share of pounding. In the early 1500s she had an extensive beach, was about a mile from the sea, and had half a dozen streets the shore side of the Moot Hall. These streets are now lost. Records show that over time they were abandoned because of constant flooding and erosion, and the Moot Hall is now no longer in the centre of town, but next to the sea.

Aldeburgh being pounded by the sea
(Suffolk Record Office, ref. K646/8)

The Moot Hall, Aldeburgh
(Suffolk Record Office, ref. PT003/4)

THE CHANGING SUFFOLK COAST

Devastation at Thorpeness
(Suffolk Record Office, ref. K646/22)

In 1590, because of the erosion of the foreshore, the town bailiffs stated that, 'Because of the sea's daily wynneth of the land against the Towne' they forbade the locals 'to remove any stones under pain of a fine of three farthings for every offence' and their children and servants were threatened with 'imprisonment at the discretion of the Bailies'. Groynes and jetties were built to try and stop the erosion.

Up to the 1800s there was a large tidal inlet twixt Aldeburgh and Thorpeness called Thorpe Haven or The Meare. It was protected from the open sea by a shingle spit, and was a safe haven for boats in heavy and strong seas. Eventually the haven was filled in, both by man, to create polder land and farmland, and by natural causes, either by silting up from brooks and streams running in, or from longshore drift from the sea. Today, all that's left is a much smaller boating and fishing lake – but it still has kept The Meare as its name. Good! We don't want everything to disappear!

To me, perhaps the most fascinating story is the demise of Slaughden, just south of Aldeburgh. The reason why it intrigues me the most is that my late father could recall the last great storm that sounded the final death knoll for Slaughden, leaving only a small quay, one house and a Martello tower built during the Napoleonic Wars.

Slaughden had been a very busy port with a fishing fleet, a coastal fleet, warships, (five ships were sent to fight against the Armada), three quays, a boat-building industry, and all together employed some 600-odd people (they were all pretty odd in Slaughden!). Slaughden could be reached directly from the sea, or up the rivers Ore and Alde, the latter route being more protected. However, the river Alde was gradually silting up and the port began to decline. By the late 1800s Slaughden had been reduced to 100 fishing boats and 20 coastal vessels.

At the beginning of the 20th century, only 20 families remained, the sea was taking its toll, big time. On high spring tides, the people

Clearing up at Slaughden
(Suffolk Record Office, ref. K646/25)

used to open their back and front doors, to allow the tide to go in and out (one way of washing the floor clean). Gradually, one by one, the houses were lost to the sea and in 1923 the Mariners pub had to be demolished. In 1926 a great storm, and the floods which followed it, had the final say, and only one house, aptly-named The Hazard was left. (The old boy who lived there, got 'hoom' that night, and said to his wife, 'Oi've never knowed a noight like ut.')

*The last house in Slaughden –
The Hazard
(Suffolk Record Office,
ref. K681/1/3/86)*

The people of Slaughden had a nickname; they were called 'Codbangers'. (Told you they were odd.) They built unique 45-ft fishing smacks, with a well at the bottom of the boat that the sea water ran through. They would sail to far off Iceland, catch their cod and store them in the well thus keeping them alive. They would return to Slaughden, unload their catch, sit on their upturned 'maunds' (fishing baskets) and then kill the cod by hitting them on the head with a cudgel – hence the name 'codbangers'.

Today, Slaughden consists of a sea wall, one small quay, a small boat-building yard, two sailing clubs and the Martello tower.

Covehithe

This stretch of the coast is now the fastest-eroding coastline in England, with an estimated rate of ten yards (I 'hent' gone metric yet) a year. This means the 500-year-old church will go the same way as Dunwich in about 25 years' time, and the village will be under threat of extinction. Covehithe, which used to be a fair way inland, was partly protected by a shingle bar out at sea but unfortunately the bar shifted and left Covehithe exposed to the full force of the sea and the weather — the soft sandy cliffs stand no chance.

Lowestoft – Ness Point

This is now the most easterly point in the British Isles, (and Suffolk as well, of course), but that would not have been the case many years ago. It is suggested that it had gone out a lot further but, once again, the sea took it away. Now where does all this eroded land go to? 'Gotta *goo* somewhere.'

As depicted on the maps showing 'then and now', you will see the lines of longshore drift. The tides and currents come in from the north-east. The waves, especially the storm waves, erode the coast and take its load of sand and shingle straight out to sea, only for it to be brought back in again with the waves, eroding some more and taking a heavier load back out. These heavily-laden waves mean that the sea off the Suffolk coast never looks a clear blue-green but is always that murky colour. This process of longshore drift gradually takes all that material down the coast. The sea can't hold on to it forever, so when she meets the current of a river at its mouth two things tends to happen. Firstly, the sea loses momentum and dumps some of its load and, secondly, the river does likewise, offloading silt brought down from the land. This is exactly what happened with the river Alde. Over the years a massive spit formed and Orford Ness was created.

This spit now goes all the way to Shingle Street. At the same time the river was silting up, contributing to the demise of the economic well-being of Slaughden.

You will see on the map on page 93, there was no Landguard Point in Anglo-Saxon times. Once again the longshore drift met the river Orwell and gradually formed that area of land which is now the most south-easterly part of the county.

THE CHANGING SUFFOLK COAST

The Orford Ness Lighthouses (Suffolk Record Office FPT/311/1)

The River Deben

Before the Romans decided to invade our shores, the river Deben, just inland, was some four miles across. As you can see from the map (*opposite*), it had a completely different shape from that of today.

The Romans had a settlement at Walton, although they called it 'suffen' different then, and in a very limited way they started the reclamation programme of the area. They did this by 'inning' the saltings (taking in an area of marshland to create salt beds). The Angles and Saxons had a big influence on the area, and reclaimed some of the area by 'warping'. At low tide, they would 'plaunch' their way, knee deep, into a marshy area, and build a low bank of earth, sometimes constructed with faggots, (got to have a sense of humour to do that job – even a 'warped' sense of humour). When the tide starts to come in, the river slows down and floods the area they have blocked off. The river then dumps all its muddy silt. At low tide, they started the process again. It's a long haul, but they would raise the ground level by some three feet in three years, vegetation would take hold, and after ten years you've got an area of land you can do something with – the Anglo-Saxons would call this piece of land an 'ey' or 'ay'. Eventually, settlements were built on this reclaimed land, and it's fair to say, all those villages ending with 'ey', near the river Deben – Hemley, Bawdsey, Trimley, and a host more, are all built on Anglo-Saxon reclaimed land.

The Normans did their bit, building walls and reclaiming land – this carried on through the reigns of the Tudors and Stuarts, until we get the landscape of today. Many original ports and quays were lost through this reclamation – the most famous being Kingsfleet, so called because it was such a safe inland port and harbour that several kings, John, Richard, Edward and others, moored their royal fleets there. Now Kingsfleet is two miles inland.

Where Is It All Going?

The changing coastline can be explained, but it's a frightening

THE CHANGING SUFFOLK COAST

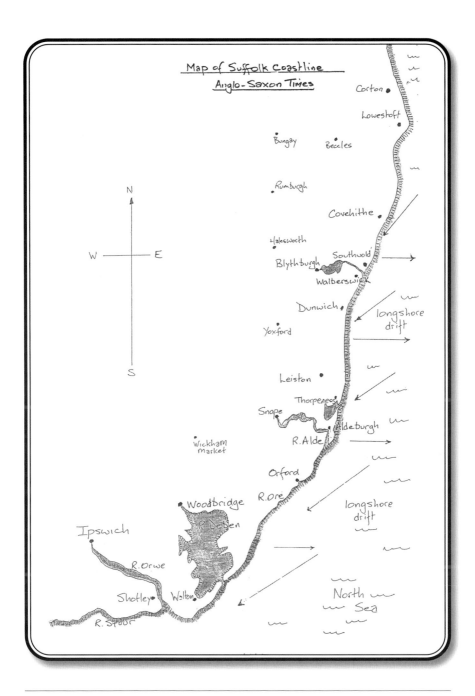

Map of Suffolk Coastline
Anglo-Saxon Times

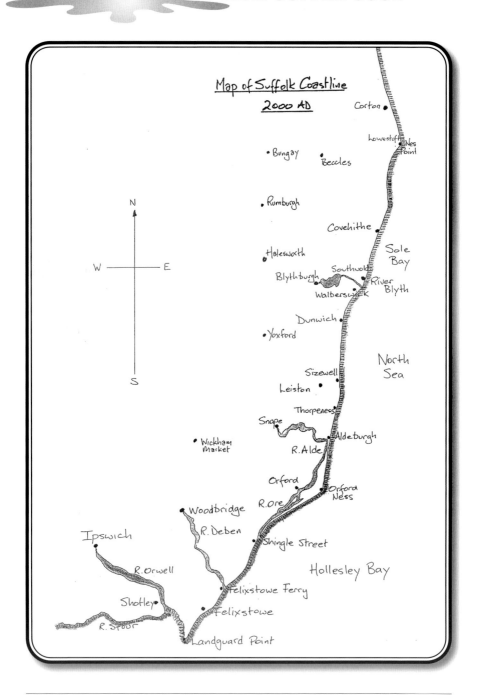

Map of Suffolk Coastline
2000 AD

Corton

Lowestoft
Ness Point

Bungay

Beccles

Rumburgh

Covehithe

Sole Bay

N

Haleswoth

Southwold

W — E

Blythburgh

River Blyth

Walberswick

S

Dunwich

Yoxford

North Sea

Sizewell

Leiston

Thorpeness

Snape

Aldeburgh

Wickham Market

R. Alde

Orford

Orford Ness

Woodbridge

R. Ore

R. Deben

Ipswich

Shingle Street

Hollesley Bay

R. Orwell

Felixstowe Ferry

Shotley

Felixstowe

R. Stour

Landguard Point

THE CHANGING SUFFOLK COAST

The 'Gulliver' wind turbine at Lowestoft
(courtesy of the Windmill House Collection)

thought when you add global warming into the equation. Suffolk has many low-lying areas, and Ipswich will get her flood barrier – approval has been passed. Unfortunately, in the long run, it will not stem the tide – remember King Canute? Not in my lifetime, but I'm sure we will one day be hearing place names like Sudbury-next-the-Sea, Needham Market Ness, Stowmarket Sands and Polstead Point. It's a sobering thought, especially when you consider the fact that Norfolk people are already gearing themselves up to losing six coastal parishes. Norfolk is not very far away!

'We doon't wont a goo th' sayme way as Norf'k!'

(The Windmill House Collection)